Humanities Matter

The Essay Collection

by AerleTaree

Cover art courtesy of Aerle Taree.

Copyright © 2007 by Aerle T. Jones for Reality Writings, Inc.
Published by Pearson Custom Publishing
All rights reserved.

Permission in writing must be obtained from the publisher before any part of this work may be reproduced or transmitted in any form or by any means, electronic or mechanical, including photocopying and recording, or by any information storage or retrieval system.

All trademarks, service marks, registered trademarks, and registered service marks are the property of their respective owners and are used herein for identification purposes only.

Printed in the United States of America

10 9 8 7 6 5 4 3 2 1

ISBN 978-0-6151-6754-1

2006540143

EC

Table of Contents

A Letter from Johnnetta Cole v

Introduction ix

PART 1: *Art History* 1
    Essay 1: Phoenix Hall 3
    Essay 2: Arena Chapel. 21

PART 2: *African American Studies* 33
    Essay 1: The Evolution of the
              Black Entertainer. 35
    Essay 2: The Harlem Renaissance 45

PART 3: *Philosophy and Linguistics* 51
    Essay 1: Ethics, Morals and a
              "Just Life" 53
    Essay 2: The Evolution of Swahili 63

PART 4: *Anthropology* 71
    Essay 1: Brief History of
              Homo sapiens 73
    Essay 2: Culture Clashes in
              Globalization. 79

Bibliography 87

A Letter from Johnnetta Cole

Dear Reader,

Over the course of the almost four decades that I have been in the academy as a professor and administrator, I have of course interacted with many students. Aerle Jones stands out among all of these students because of her many talents: her ability to set a goal and keep at it until she reaches it, her deep involvement in the world of ideas, and her passion for teaching art history.

I first met Aerle Jones in 1996. At that time she indicated her commitment to returning to school to complete her undergraduate work, to go on to do graduate work and one day to become a professor. That is the path that she has indeed followed. In 1997, Aerle enrolled at Spelman College, an institution where I served as the president from 1987 to 1997. She received her B.A. degree from Oglethorpe University in 2003. It was a long journey for Aerle Jones to complete her undergraduate degree, but she did, and it stands as a prime example of her tenacity.

As a young woman, Aerle Jones was highly successful in the world of popular music. She was the "mastermind" behind the successful activities of the popular group, Arrested Development. While with that group, she won two Grammy Awards, an MTV Moon Man award, and two NAACP Image awards. What impressed me when I first met Ms. Jones is that she was convinced that with all of the visibility and monetary rewards that she was receiving as an artist, published poet, businesswoman and president of a music publishing company, her "real calling" was to become a professor. She is quite an intellectual in the sense that she is constantly reading and thinking and playing with ideas; she truly enjoys figuring out problems; she is skilled as a researcher; and she truly is in love with writing.

Johnnetta Cole, Ph.D.
Bennett College
President

United Way
Chairman

Introduction

Humanities matters in modern society, and impacts our lives in subtle and not-so-subtle ways. On television you may see a woman in a war-torn country cry out, "Where's the humanity?" She asks a fine question, indeed, yet not a particularly easy one to answer. Change the channel and the newscaster reports a sliver of humanity—the opening of a center to help people with dyslexia and language-based learning differences, dedicated by Bill and Camille Cosby on behalf of the Hello Friend/Ennis William Cosby Foundation, which they established in memory of their late son.

In spite of our fast-paced lives in a global financial marketplace (driven primarily from internet and technological advances), the issue of caring for mankind still remains a top priority. To foster an understanding and appreciation of the humanities, I have gathered this collection of my writings. My hope is that *Humanities Matters* will help you to better understand the principles of social interaction, historical behavior, and human and humanistic development.

These essays should encourage discussion and information sharing. To gain the most from your *Humanities Matters* experience I recommend that you cross reference the materials cited in the bibliography. I have developed this text to be accessible to both professional scholars and first-time humanities students.

Researching and writing these essays became a large part of my advanced education, culminating in receiving my bachelor's degree in humanities, with a focus on art, from Oglethorpe University. While taking studio classes at Oglethorpe, I created the artwork on the cover of this book. May you derive pleasure and enjoyment from the cover art, as well as the content herein.

I owe special thanks to Johnnetta B. Cole, current president of Bennett College, for writing the letter that appears at the front of *Humanities Matters*. In 1987, Dr. Cole made history by becoming the first African American women to serve as President of Spelman College. She is one of the nation's foremost scholars in the humanities, an anthropology professor and an outstanding academic administrator, and I am extremely grateful for her encouragement and positive message.

What you do with the ideas and information presented in *Humanities Matters* is entirely up to you. My sincere hope is that you find the essays thought-provoking and enlightening, and that they serve as a springboard to further your continued education in the humanities.

Aerle T. Jones
Atlanta, Georgia
November, 2006

PART 1:

Art History

Essay 1

Phoenix Hall

You enter the gates as a large garden unfolds before your eyes. There is a pond beyond the garden. Across the waters you see a multi-story temple that appears to have a golden Buddha floating inside. It is 8:30 a.m. and the gates have just opened; you have until 5:15 p.m. to take in the sights of the world famous Phoenix Hall of Byodoin Temple. As you reach in your wallet to pay the 600-yen admission fee, you notice the image of the Temple on the Japanese 10 yen coin. You may not know that the Temple was originally built as a villa for the famous Fujiwara family; in fact, you may not know much about the beautiful Phoenix Hall of Byodoin Temple located in Uji, Japan, but rest assured, for I shall be your guide. I shall make certain that you get a description of the artistic aesthetics of the temple, a thorough description of the Phoenix Hall grounds, and a brief introduction to the foundational tenets of the Pure Land Buddha sect. You will discover the history of the Amida Buddha and other "Jocho Styles" of art work, the history of the Fujiwara family. You shall also receive a general overview of Japanese art history and other Japanese Temples.

Let us start by taking a look at the U-shaped compound of the Phoenix Hall. In the center of the compound is the main hall, designed to appear to have multi-stories as described in the sutras. Inside the main hall is the Amida Buddha, which was designed by the famous Japanese artist Jocho and the last remaining piece credited to him. The

> *You may not know much about the beautiful Phoenix Hall of Byodoin Temple located in Uji, Japan, but rest assured, for I shall be your guide...*

Amida Buddha is the Buddha worshipped by people of the Pure Land Sect of Buddhism. In the main hall with the Amida Buddha, there once were 52 Bodhisattvas with clouds and halos hanging from the ceiling of the hall, with each individual figure 15 to 34 inches tall. Carved out of single pieces of cypress, they are shown dancing, singing, and meditating. Of the 52, 51 of the Bodhisattvas are now classified as national treasures. Also inside the main hall of Phoenix Hall are colorful painted doors. On top of the building sit two bronze phoenixes called hoos. Attached to the main hall is the Kannondo, or Avalokitesvara Hall, considered an important representation of the Heian Period (794–1185). The main hall is flanked by two L-shaped corridors that give the suggestion of a phoenix spreading its wings. Each corridor is 9 meters from north to south and swoops eastward toward the pond at the end. Behind the main hall there is a tail corridor that is 18.4 meters long. Originally this corridor had earthen floors, but since it was rebuilt decades ago it now has wooden floors and kato style windows. There is a bell at Phoenix Hall that is ordained a national treasure due to its beautiful, elaborate design and is considered one of the three finest bells in Japan.

> *51 of the Bodhisattvas are now classified as national treasures ...*

Unlike Western art, nature plays a prominent role in Eastern Japanese art. For example, Phoenix Hall has a garden and pond that are part of the compound. Although the Ajiike pond—or the Pure Land Treasure Pond—was originally meant to be spiritual, it also served as a fire breaker during the civil war of 1336 A.D. and saved the Phoenix Hall from being razed. The pond was built so that one could see the heavenly reflections of the surroundings. The beach of the pond is said to symbolize the banks of the Uji River. A majestic mountainous backdrop stands beyond the pond. Two bridges, Soribashi, an arched bridge, and Hirabashi, a flat bridge, have been restored to how they would have appeared in the Heian Period, and connect the main hall and the garden.

The pond was built so that one could see the heavenly reflections of the surroundings. The beach of the pond is said to symbolize the banks of the Uji River.

* * *

The Byodoin Temple is a Buddhist Temple. Buddhism was introduced to Japan more than 1500 years ago. The first Buddha believed that life was suffering and that one could reach the state of nirvana by overcoming one's desires. He reached enlightenment for the first time while sitting under a bodhi tree in the Deer Park of India. Buddhism underwent many transformations before it reached Japan. The Japanese Buddhists believed that the Chinese phoenix bird was the protector of Buddha. When introduced to Japan, Buddhism began to form sects; one of the more popular Buddhist sects to emerge was the Jodo of Pure Land sect during the Heian Period. It was during the practice of this religion that the Amida (also, Amitabha) Buddha began to be worshipped and enshrined. The Pure Land Buddhist believed that Amida promised to create a paradise where all Buddhists could rest in the afterlife. In paradise one could focus on becoming enlightened and be free from the suffering of the earthly world. The environment of this paradise was filled with lovely music, cool water, jeweled trees, singing birds, and fragrant air. The Phoenix Hall of Temple Byodoin is the realization of the Amida Buddha's paradise and an effort to try to recreate it on earth.

> The Pure Land Buddhist believed that Amida promised to create a paradise where all Buddhists could rest in the afterlife.

Inside the main hall of Phoenix Hall is a large carved wooden statue of the Amida Buddha. The sculpture is more than nine feet tall in the traditional seated position. The entire figure is done in gold leaf, beneath which is a black lacquer finish. As the sculpture is too large to have come from one tree, it was created in an innovative joined-wood construction style called the yosegi-zukuri technique credited to the artist Jocho. The hands of the Amida Buddha are shaped in spiritual hand gestures, or mudras. He has a compassionate facial expression and a gently contoured body. His hair is in neat and orderly curls. The eyes of the Amida Buddha are half closed, giving him a serene look. The reason the Amida seems to be floating on air when viewed from across the water of the pond may be due to raigo, or the "welcoming descent of Amida." It is said that Amida vowed to personally come at the second of death to help transport an individual safely to the Pure Land paradise.

Three factors made Jocho's style unique. First, wood was used in the creation of his pieces. Second, Jocho developed the joined-wood construction called the yosegi-zukuri technique from the prior single woodblock construction called the ichiboku-zukuri technique. And third, Jocho-style pieces could be mass-produced by a team of sculptors in a workshop, with Jocho as the master applying only the finishing touches. Pure Land Buddhists created a huge demand for Amida Buddha sculptures by teaching that one could simply achieve nirvana by chanting the name of Amida Buddha. In other words, "It may have been the popularity of this sect that led people to want all the statues before which they prayed to look the same" (Satoshi, 1). Jocho, and the other artists who adopted his style, tried to meet that demand. It is said that Jocho once produced 27 life-size statues of Buddha in 54 days with the help of 100 other artists. These figures were placed in temples like the Mibu-Dera Temple in Kyoto. Amida Buddha believers believed that the size of the Buddha that they prayed to affected the manner in which they were transported to Pure Land paradise. An Amida Buddha such as the one at the Phoenix Hall of Byodoin Temple would ensure that one was transferred to paradise in luxury.

> *Pure Land Buddhists created a huge demand for Amida Buddha sculptures by teaching that one could simply achieve nirvana by chanting the name of Amida Buddha.*

Popular images of the Amida Buddha other than Jocho-style sculptures were Amida mandalas, which are spiritual drawings of geometric symbols and patterns, usually representing the cosmos. In mandalas, the Amida Buddha was often shown sitting on a lotus flower or beneath a jeweled canopy. Like leaders of other religions, his body would be gold to represent the light that was supposed to radiate from inside his body, and he is depicted surrounded by musicians and Bodhisattvas. Bodhisattvas are individuals who have attained enlightenment in the Buddhist religion but who have refused nirvana because of their great compassion and desire to help others along the path of enlightenment.

* * *

The Japanese royal family can be traced back to Amaterasu, the sun goddess in the Shinto religion. The first emperor's name meant "Son of Heaven." This is reflected in Japanese art as well, where Shinto deities became manifestations of the Buddha. However, even the divine imperial lineage would prove to be no match for the Fujiwara family's influence. It is difficult to pinpoint exactly when this powerful and extremely politically savvy clan began asserting their influence on the throne, but they are generally regarded as being the power behind the throne from approximately 794–1160 A.D. The Fujiwara influence was strongest during the last half of the Heian Period, or the peace and tranquility period. In 858 A.D., Fujiwara Yoshifusa, the Grand Minister, made his grandson the Emperor and appointed himself as regent for a minor, or sessho. Later Fujiwara Mototsune, Yoshifusa's nephew, acted as regent to the adult emperor, or kampaku.

The Emperor Daigo (897–930 A.D.) was able to put the Fujiwara reign in check for a short while, and ruled directly. But as Emperor Daigo ruled, the Fujiwara estate became more wealthy and eventually more powerful, acquiring large swaths of land, known as shoen, throughout Japan. Over time, shoens gained legal status and were given privileges such as tax breaks and exemptions from government inspections. These were similar to the Japanese fief and English manorial systems, except the farm workers held a legal share in a farm's profits and harvests whereas the serfs did not. Due to these changes, it became advantageous for small landowners to transfer their titles to the shoen in return for a share of the harvest.

The Fujiwara influence was strongest during the last half of the Heian Period, or the peace and tranquility period.

Regardless, within decades of Emperor Daigo's death, the Fujiwara family regained complete control of the government. The capital of Japan was moved to Kyoto to undermine the power that the Chinese-based Buddhist monks had over the Japanese government. In Uji, a small town 30 minutes south of Kyoto, Fujiwara no Michinaga built a private family villa.

Michinaga lived from 966–1027 A.D. and was considered the most influential man of his time, completely in control of the Japanese throne. His influence over the government was gained by marrying his daughters and relatives to Japanese Emperors and noblemen. Four of his daughters were married to Emperors; as well, two of his nephews and three grandchildren were Emperors. During this time, all government affairs and finances became Fujiwara household matters. The Fujiwara family became so powerful that they had their own class: only those with Fujiwara blood were considered kampaku, the highest level of the Kuge class. One member of the Fujiwara family who held the position of kampaku was Fujiwara Yorimichi. In 1053 A.D., Yori-michi, Michinaga's son, transformed his father's villa at Uji into the Buddhist Temple Byodoin.

> *The capital of Japan was moved to Kyoto to undermine the power that the Chinese-based Buddhist monks had over the Japanese government.*

Although Michinaga was the most powerful Fujiwara family member, Murasaki Shikibu is the most popular. She was born in 973 A.D. to Fujiwara Tametoki and his wife—though it is speculated that her given name was actually Fujiwara Takako, and Murasaki (the Japanese word for purple) was based on a character in her book, The Tale of Genji. Her father Tametoki was a successful man and had a long career as officer to the imperial court. He was a Chinese scholar who first sat on the Board of Ceremony, or Shikibu, and finally was appointed the governor of the Echizen province. Contrary to Japanese tradition during the

Heian Period, Murasaki was educated alongside her brothers, learning Chinese, then the official language of the imperial court. While in her twenties, Murasaki married Fujiwara no Nobutaka, a distant relative who served as a lieutenant in the Imperial Guard. After he died in 1001 she joined the Imperial Court and served as the lady in waiting for the Empress Akiko.

Murasaki was educated alongside her brothers, learning Chinese, then the official language of the imperial court.

While on the court, Murasaki began a diary and a novel called *The Tale of Genji*, considered to be the first novel ever published in the history of the world. Written somewhere between 1001–1010 A.D., *The Tale of Genji* has 54 chapters and almost four hundred characters. The main character is the son of an Emperor who is placed in the non-royal Genji clan so that he will not be a threat to anyone. The boy grows up to be intelligent and handsome, and the book tells of his many love affairs. It is a remarkable novel, written with little to no semblance of a plot and no character names (using a nobleperson's real name was considered a transgression in the culture of the court). Reflecting on the genesis of *The Tale of Genji* and the topic of what defines a novel, one critic says,

> "I have a theory of my own about what this art of the novel is and how it came into being. To begin with, it does not simply consist of the author's telling a story about the adventures of some other person. On the contrary, it happens because one's own experience of

people and things has moved one to an emotion so passionate that it can no longer be shut up in one's own heart. Again and again something in one's own life or in the lives of those around one will seem so important that the thought of letting it pass into oblivion is unbearable. There must never come a time, one feels, when people do not know about it. That is my view of how this art arose." (Reese, 3)

Ironically the downfall of the Fujiwara family came due to their strength and the source of their wealth: their land. As the wealth and privileges of the shoen grew, the common people began to despise the shoen establishments. Adopted from a practice of some Buddhist temples that had armed monks, or acuso, the wealthy began to hire Japanese warriors to defend their land. These warriors were called samurai. The samurai slowly began to take advantage of their clout with the wealthy. Ultimately, the samurai gained control of the emperor. After a nine year war and a three year war, Fujiwara Kiyohira ruled the Oshu district in northeastern Japan, known at the time as the Northern Fujiwara region. He was a distant relative of the earlier, more powerful Fujiwara family. The reign ended in 1189 when his grandson Fujiwara no Yasuhira was defeated by the forces of Minamoto no Yoritomo and thus marked the end of the Fujiwara clan's reign and the beginning of the supremacy of the samurai and the ascension of the military class.

> *Ultimately, the samurai gained control of the emperor.*

The modern day Fujiwara family has dissolved but they are not forgotten. There is an annual Spring Fujiwara Festival in Japan each May 1. During the festival, scenes from the Heian Period are reenacted and hundreds gather for a parade where celebrity guests dress up as Yoshitsune riding on white horses.

* * *

To understand exactly how the Phoenix Hall of Byodoin Temple fits into the scheme of the Japanese landscape, lets take a closer look at Japanese art history, starting with the pre-historic Jomon Period (10,000 B.C. – 300 B.C.). Archaeologists credit early Japanese with producing the world's first pottery vessels during this period, which gets its name from jomon, meaning "cord-marked," as many clay and pottery vessels and figurines of the time were stylized with cord impressions. In the following Yayoi period we begin to see geometric shapes on the pottery. Bell-shaped bronzes called dotaku were also made during this time. Dotakus are believed to have derived from Korean musical instruments that symbolized authority.

Archaeologists credit early Japanese with producing the world's first pottery vessels

The Chinese Tang Dynasty had a large influence over the art and culture of the Nara Period, including the adoption of Chinese characters and the spread of Buddhism. This meant that structure was dominant over ornamentation. In the Heian Period that would follow,

Chinese art became assimilated into the culture and "Japanized." We begin to see buildings being constructed that are highly decorative like the Phoenix Hall of Byodoin Temple. Other art pieces created throughout this time are yamato-e style paintings; emaji, or illustrated scrolls that unfold to poetry or prose; and nise-e portraits. As is generally the case in a society experiencing a dearth of wealth and leisure, more time and effort can be spent on art and other aesthetically pleasing aspects of life. Thus, many of the works of art were highly fashionable products of the rich court life that existed during the Heian period.

The Muromachi Period would see the rise of such famous Japanese art forms as Karesansui, or meaningful gardens, more commonly known as Japanese rock gardens. Shoin-zukuri architecture, a style based on Zen monastic dwellings, would replace the Muromachi Period's shinden-zukuri; and of course, the tea ceremony developed, introduced from China and developed an aesthetic unique to Japan.

The Azuchi-Momoyama Period is named after the samurai castles Azuchi and Momoyama. Also during this time a type of architecture based on the tea ceremony, sukiya-zukuri, became popular; this was a minimalist style in stark contrast with the previous styles. In the following period of Edo we begin to see rippa paintings of heavy pigment; maki-e, or gold ornament lacquer design; bunjinga,

Japanese ink paintings influenced by China's Ming Dynasty; and ukiyo-e, woodblock prints of everyday life.

* * *

Temples like the Phoenix Hall of Byodoin are dedicated to the worship of Buddha. They are places where monks and nuns train, live, and study and where worshippers come to meditate, chant, and pray. There are many different features in a Japanese Temple. There is the to (pagoda), kondo or hondo (main hall), kodo (lecture hall), shoro (bell tower), kyozo (sutra depository), sobo (dormitory), and jikido (dining hall).

As described earlier, the Phoenix Hall of Byodoin Temple is a former villa. An example of another villa-temple is the Horyuji Temple, also known as Horyu Gakumonji or Learning Temple of the Flourishing Law. Built in 607 A.D. in Ikaruga, Horyuji was originally a retirement retreat for the prince regent Shotoku Taisihi. Shotoku Taisihi was the first to establish Buddhism as a state religion in Japan. After his death, his followers honored his memory by turning the villa into a Buddhist Temple. The Horyuji Temple is comprised of an East and West Precinct, and each Precinct has a courtyard that is aligned to a north-south axis.

* * *

Neither Amida Hall of Kosanji Templ, nor Byodo-in Temple in the Valley of the Temples on the island of Oahu, Hawaii, are not to be confused with the Phoenix Hall of Byodoin Temple, though they are both modeled after the great shrine. The Kosanji Temple is unique in that it is without a congregation, built by Kosanji Koso I after the death of his mother. Construction started prior to World War II but was not completed for nearly thirty years. This Temple has 25 Bodhisattva carvings on either side of the doorway. Inside the Temple is a Buddhist altar, colorfully decorated in gold leaf. To the right and left of the altar are sculptures of the Goddess of Mercy. The Goddess of Mercy statues were received from the Kofukuji Temple in Nara, Japan. Above the altar on the ceiling is a masterpiece by painter Kawakami Setsui, depicting dragons twisted in clouds.

> *The Kosanji Temple is unique in that it is without a congregation.*

* * *

Now you have a brief glimpse into the tremendous history that stands behind the Phoenix Hall of Byodoin Temple. If this subject interests you, you are encouraged to read further on Japan's art history, its temples, Jocho's pioneering style of work and the Amida Buddha statue. Never fear: there is more intrigue behind the political triumphs and eventual downfall of the Fujiwara clan than could be covered here. Buddhism remains a fascinating system of beliefs, and the Pure Land sect of Buddhism is an exemplary example. So after taking in the

> *Buddhism remains a fascinating system of beliefs, and the Pure Land sect of Buddhism is an exemplary example.*

sights and reflecting on your day at 116 Ujirenge, Uji-shi, Kyoto, 611–0021, grab a handful of pamphlets—make sure they're printed in English—and prepare for the 10 minute walk back to the Uji Station on the Keihan line.

Essay 2

Arena Chapel

Art is said to be the window to the soul, and in the case of the Cappella degli Scrovegni—built over the site of a Roman arena better known as Arena Chapel—this statement is quite true. The chapel walls are covered with frescoes created by Giotto di Bondone (1267–1337) and is considered to be one of the best examples of the technique as well as one of the most important works in Western Art.

Renaissance scholars would argue that Giotto's work represents the beginning of the Renaissance-style of painting.

A fresco is a painting made on wet plaster, and then allowed to dry. It is a point of contention among Medieval and Renaissance scholars as to which period Giotto belonged. Technically the years in which he worked are considered the Medieval period, Renaissance scholars would argue that his work represents the beginning of the Renaissance-style of painting, especially with the influence his work—specifically the Arena Chapel—had on such Renaissance artists as Michelangelo, as can be seen in the Sistine Chapel.

Giotto was paid handsomely for his work on Arena Chapel and was quite a wealthy man, earning most of his money through investments in the silk industry. Giotto was born near Florence in the town of Colle di Vespignano, the son of a farmer. He was well-traveled; commissions for his work took him to Rome, Padua, Arezzo, Rimini, Assisi, and Naples. Giorgio Vasari, one of Giotto's first biographers, tells of how a well-known Florentine painter by the name of Cimabue discovered Giotto's talents. Cimabue supposedly saw the 12-year-old boy sketching one of his father's sheep on a flat rock and was so impressed with his talent that he persuaded the father to let Giotto become his pupil. But that may be of doubtful authenticity, as there is another story where Giotto, while apprenticed to a wool merchant in Florence, frequented Cimabue's studio so much that he was finally allowed to study painting.

Vasari also tells a story of how Pope Benedict XI sent a messenger to Giotto, requesting a sample of his work. Giotto dipped his brush in red and with one continuous stroke painted a perfect circle, assuring the messenger that the worth of this sample would be recognized and urging him to return to the Pope with that message. When the Pope saw the painting he was indeed pleased and commissioned Giotto to adorn the walls of the papal residence in Avignon, France. In 1334, the city of Florence honored Giotto with the title of Magnus Magister (Great Master) and appointed him City Architect and Superintendent of Public Works. The writer Dante Alighieri even praised him, writing in the The Divine Comedy that Giotto had surpassed the talents of his master, Cimabue.

Giotto dipped his brush in red and with one continuous stroke painted a perfect circle...

Giotto's masterpiece, the Arena Chapel, was commissioned by the banker Enrico Scrovegni. Some have argued that Scrovegni's motivation for having the chapel painted came from his father, who had been jailed for wrongdoings. Riginaldo made his fortune by lending money at exorbitant interest rates. In the modern era it is considered the practice of banking, but in the Medieval period it was considered a sin, and Dante has placed him in the seventh circle of Hell in The Divine Comedy. While it is thought that Enrico Scrovegni built the chapel to help atone for his father's sins, it may be that he had his own atonements in mind, as he is represented in the painting of the Last Judgment. At the time, Pope Boniface VIII was granting complete pardon to all sins (provided they were confessed), including such sins as these money-lending practices. Scrovegni eventually received absolution from Pope Benedict XI. The purchase of the chapel could have been one of the terms of the absolution.

The Arena Chapel was mostly a family oratory, and was dedicated to Santa Maria della Carita, the Virgin of Charity.

Scrovegni's family consisted of his mother Cappellina, his wife, and his four daughters. The Arena Chapel was mostly a family oratory, and was dedicated to Santa Maria della Carita, the Virgin of Charity. Charity is depicted in the virtues shown on the south wall of the Arena Chapel. Crowned with roses, she holds a bowl laden with nature's bounty: lilies, roses, poppies, corn, pomegranates, and wheat. This characterization of Charity is different from that of earlier Italian depictions. Those painters would not have associated her with fertility as Giotto did. Underlining the association with the annunciated virgin, the Arena Chapel's dedication ceremony on March 25, 1303, was performed on the Feast of the Annunciation.

The kind of ceremony that usually took place inside the Arena Chapel was the Golden Mass. During the Medieval

Period, the Golden Mass included actors who would play out stories from the scriptures. Young boys would play the Virgin Mary and other women depicted in the bible. Clergy would read their sermons as musical arrangements and dramatic embellishments would take place in the foreground. During Giotto's lifetime, there was a transformation where paintings began to replace the actors. We can begin to deduce that Giotto's frescoes on the chapel walls held special meaning. They were responsible for educating the masses during the religious ceremonies that took place inside the building; however, as literacy grew, the clergy was pushed to the forefront and the paintings became a backdrop to the Mass.

The frescoes that Giotto chose to cover the walls of the Arena Chapel are based on a book entitled **The Golden Legend.**

The frescoes that Giotto chose to cover the walls of the Arena Chapel are based on a book entitled *The Golden Legend*. This book has no connection to the Golden Mass, which was performed in the chapel. With tales of Jesus on the left wall and the Virgin Mary on the right wall, Giotto grounded the scenes on writings from the book. An example is the story of Joachim and Anna. In *The Golden Legend* it is stated, "It was not proper for a sterile man...to stand among men who begot sons." Joachim was thus exiled, and Giotto painted the scene "Joachim Takes Refuge in the Wilderness" on the chapel walls.

Compiled around 1260 by Jacobus de Voragine, the Dominican archbishop of Genoa, The Golden Legend is a collection of hagiographies that brings to life encounters of ancient and medieval saints. His writing was so popular that it exceeded the bible in numbers printed before the 1500s. Stories in *The Golden Legend* often sound familiar; for example, the story of "The Seven Sleepers" sounds suspiciously like a medieval version of Rip Van Winkle, and a spun-out story of Judas included in the chapter on St. Matthew is reminiscent of Oedipus. Regardless of their familiarity, Giotto and other educated people of the Renaissance and Medieval periods diligently read the stories of The Golden Legend.

* * *

The practice of lending money at high interest rates is called usury, and Giotto made it one of the main themes of his paintings in the Arena Chapel. Like his father Riginaldo, Scrovegni himself was also actively involved in the condemned practice of usury, and all its negative spiritual connotations. At the time it was considered not only socially disruptive, but metaphysically subversive behavior. In the frescoes of the Arena Chapel and in Medieval theology, there is a connection between usury and forbidden sexuality. The Church takes action against usurers as it does against other thieves, for they engage in the public trade of usury in order to earn a living. Similarly, the Church takes action against prostitutes, who offend God by carrying

The practice of lending money at high interest rates is called usury

on prostitution as a trade by which they maintain their livelihood. Inheriting a usurer's wealth was doubly problematic, as sons could not retain any of the wealth that their fathers accumulated by means of usury.

The Church takes action against usurers as it does against other thieves, for they engage in the public trade of usury in order to earn a living.

Wives played a major role in all matters relating to usury. The wife of a usurer would strive to persuade her husband to renounce his cursed trade and return the money. A dutiful wife's obligations continued even after the death of her sinful spouse. Through assiduous prayer, widows might ensure their husbands' salvation.

Although the Golden Mass of the Arena Chapel included much artificial lighting, the architecture of the building also includes natural lighting that Giotto attempted to use in accentuating the figures of his frescoes. One effect of the natural light created by Giotto can be observed just before ten o'clock in the morning. A single sunbeam enters the Chapel through the tracery of a window in the south wall and traverses the otherwise shaded surface of the west wall. It travels diagonally down the wall to the scene of the chapel's Dedication and passes between Scrovegni's outstretched hands. Built into the original design of the building, shutters were integral to the windows of the south wall. On the west wall, high in the center of the Last Judgment, the halo of Christ the Judge reflects light from its level. The north wall has no windows at all.

Giotto tried to make the characters of the Arena Chapel frescoes as lifelike as possible, paying close attention to details such as clothing and facial expressions. There is in fact much in the frescoes that reflects Giotto's detailed observation of dress code, fashion, and even dressmaking techniques. For instance, in several scenes from "The Life of the Virgin," the practice of gathering the supertinical (female religious vestments) up at the front when venturing outdoors is shown. This rendering involved an arrangement of looped cords attached to the front hem of the garment, which could be raised or lowered like a swagged window curtain. In the fresco "The Meeting at the Golden Gate," Giotto shows a small slit in Saint Anne's garment underneath the armhole that allows access to the mechanism that operates the supertunicale. In the fresco the "Annunciation," the Archangel Gabriel wears a white garment with gold trimmings. That type of white vestment, often seen in the chapel, was frequently worn by cleric-actors playing angels during ceremonies. Such attention to detail confirms that Giotto had begun the transformation to Renaissance art. In Medieval times, artists were less inclined to give their subjects human qualities. In fact, the opposite would happen: the artist would try to depict their characters as Gothic, larger than life figures.

It is this rejection of Gothic artistic styles that causes Giotto to be regarded as the founder of central, traditional

> *There is in fact much in the frescoes that reflects Giotto's detailed observation of dress code, fashion, and even dressmaking techniques.*

Western painting. He rejected the bright, jewel-like colors and long, elegant lines of the Byzantine style in favor of a quieter, more realistic presentation. Giotto's scenes break with rigid Medieval stylization to present human figures in rounded sculptural forms that appear to have been based on living models rather than on idealized archetypes. In this area, Giotto was quite ahead of his time. His example was crucial to the development of later Florentine painting and his preoccupation with the realities of the human figure and visible world became the dominant concerns of the Florentine Renaissance.

Giotto painted 38 frescoes on the Arena Chapel walls. Over the archway of the choir is a scene of "The Court of Heaven." The west wall is covered with "The Last Judgment." Over the chancel arch, there is the "Annunciation." The main wall areas have three tiers of paintings representing scenes from the life of the Virgin Mary, her parents St. Anne and St. Joachim, and Christ. Below these scenes are figures personifying virtues and vices.

At first glance, a number of the frescoes that Giotto painted in the Arena Chapel reveal a certain Renaissance flair. For instance, on the right side of his Nativity scene, there are two men standing with their backs towards the viewer. This is a first for Medieval art. In one piece, Giotto has the body of one of the men coming out of the frame, and he uses other tricks of the eye throughout, attempting to show true motion on the part of his figures. In the

"Last Judgment" scene, where Enrico Scrovegni offers a model of the Arena Chapel to the Virgin Mary, the painting seems to suggest that the model actually has weight in his hands. And with this important fresco came the introduction of weight and gravity. In frescoes prior to Giotto, figures appeared weightless as though they were floating in air. We also begin to see lifelike background features in the frescoes; in "Joachim Takes Refuge in the Wilderness," there are trees and rocks, heretofore unseen in other frescoes.

At first glance, a number of the frescoes that Giotto painted in the Arena Chapel reveal a certain Renaissance flair.

Giotto places his figures in environments in which everyday people can relate. In the "Apparition to Saint Anne," the angel descends into a well-illuminated, recognizably domestic interior, furnished and equipped for a comfortable, everyday life. The fresco readily illustrates Giotto's interest in expanding the narrative effect of his art through the inclusion of realistic detail. The artist's visualization of the scene shows the angel arriving through a high window. This bears a similarity to the staging of the "Annunciation" in some church dramas.

On the west wall of Arena Chapel sits the fresco of the "Last Judgment." This scene is full of opposites: Christ, radiant and lofty, versus Satan, in the shadowy depths; below Christ, the Elect to his right versus the Damned to his left; the devoutly kneeling patron Scrovegni versus the hanged traitor Judas. That particular use of biblical imagery draws a direct parallel between greed and damnation.

Indeed, Judas and several of the other damned are hanged by the strings of moneybags tied around their necks. Judas's suicide in the "Last Judgment" shows fulfillment of the prophecy in the Meditations, and another fertility reference: "What you have conceived, you will bear." Giotto's depiction of the suicide is different from traditional representations. What distinguishes Giotti's version from other depictions is the way in which Judas dies. In Florence, Judas merely hangs, but in Padua his viscera spill out of his body. There are other torturers in this scene: near Satan's left hip a scaly green monster gnaws on one man's penis, and above them a black demon grabs another man's genitals. Hanging to the right are four of the damned suspended by their genitals.

Judas's suicide in the "Last Judgment" shows fulfillment of the prophecy in the Meditations, and another fertility reference: "What you have conceived, you will bear."

Although Giotto lived and worked during what is widely accepted as the Medieval era, it becomes increasingly clear that he had one foot in the door of the Renaissance. His paintings were influenced by Gothic writings; a theme of Gothic civilization underlies his work, and the styles depicted in his frescoes are considered refreshing and innovative for their time. We deem Giotto a master of his craft, and the Arena Chapel to be one of his finest masterpieces. If well preserved, people will be able to view the works of Giotto for generations to come.

PART 2:

African American Studies

Essay 1

The Evolution of the Black Entertainer

People in the African American community who are talented in music or sports have always been considered special. Even during the time of slavery, the black men who were privileged to be excused from working in the field were those who entertained the slave masters by singing and dancing, or in more extreme cases, fighting other slaves for sport. Consider the fact that Bill Gates, the wealthiest man in this country, is in the technical field of computers, whereas today's wealthiest black people, Oprah Winfrey and Michael Jordan, are in sports and entertainment professions. African American children who want to grow up and be financially well off usually have the goal of being professional ball players, singers or rap artists. But unlike the generations that preceded them, in order to achieve this goal they don't have to abandon all aspirations of having a traditionally stable and healthy family life. Through the lens of such issues as the social construction of gender, the economic basis of social status, and marriage and family life in historical and modern times, this reading analyzes the impact that the lifestyle of entertainers, and more specifically the lifestyle of singers, has had on the African American community.

African American children who want to grow up and be financially well off usually have the goal of being professional ball players, singers or rap artists.

A legend to many, a mystery to all, and considered the grandfather of rock and roll, Robert Leroy Johnson (May 8, 1911–August 16, 1938) lived a short life on the roads of the south as a traveling musician. The British supergroup Cream covered Johnson's song "Cross Road Blues", and many other contemporary rock bands credit Johnson with their sound and style, from Jimi Hendrix and Led Zeppelin, to Bob Dylan and The Rolling Stones, to The White Stripes and Red Hot Chili Peppers.

The documentary *The Search for Robert Johnson* (1992), depicts him as a womanizing nomad. Although he was twice married, marriage was not an institution that would fully allow him to express his art. Marriage forced him to forego his free-wheeling blues-driven lifestyle for a sedentary one of manual labor and working the fields. Indeed, for the majority of his life, Robert Johnson was a traveling blues artist, playing on street corners and entertaining the passers-by with his electric personality. Playing the blues was the only constant in his life. As he traveled from town to town, he would make new friends and acquaintances, and new lovers-some of whom were married. It was said he often would assume different names upon arriving in a new town to hide his scandalous past. His past soon caught up with him, however, as his death outside of Greenwood, Mississippi, in 1938 came allegedly in the form of a poisoned drink from the husband of one of his lovers.

> *It was said Robert Johnson often would assume different names upon arriving in a new town to hide his scandalous past.*

As agricultural work was the main source of income in the South for the majority of black men during this period, communities shunned men like Robert Johnson who chose other occupations, classifying them as low class and unfit to marry or support a family. The men whose jobs required them to travel introduced a new kind of romantic relationship into black society, redefining the roles of men and women. Although they were involved, the women were forced to be economically independent; and although they were attached, the men were allowed to be more sexually promiscuous.

Robert Johnson's life as a blues singer was filled with many cities, many shows, and many women. His songs were filled with confessions of love and stories of heartache. The faces of his lovers who were interviewed in the documentary *The Search for Robert Johnson* express much pain and hurt.

> *It is said that in order to truly sing the blues one must sell one's soul to the devil, and that idea is certainly a part of the legend of Robert Johnson.*

When judged to the standards of higher education and pious religious belief, the life of a blues traveler was looked upon as being demonic. It is said that in order to truly sing the blues one must sell one's soul to the devil, and that idea is certainly a part of the legend of Robert Johnson. When standing at the crossroads, where one must choose their direction in life, the blues singer had to decide to walk the path that was lonely and painful. And yet the blues singer's sacrifice brought the black community a step closer to liberation. Robert Johnson and his colleagues created a social class that was of higher social status than any previously known to black men at the time.

The practice of Black Feminism could have helped the situation of the female population during this formative era in black society. Black Feminism was a reaction to and general discontent with the Civil Rights movement and the Feminist movement of the 1970s, and strives for the eradication of racism, sexism and class oppression. One of the fundamental tenets of Black Feminist theory is the idea that by sharing knowledge of their experiences, women become collectively more conscious of their situation. If the women in the South at the time would have spoken to each other more about their experiences with the new generation of blues singers who came and went like the wind, leaving a string of broken hearts, they could have empowered themselves to overcome the abusive womanizing paradigm. Ultimately they could have established a new epistemology for interacting with men who chose this non-traditional work that demanded travel and resulted in instability.

> One of the fundamental tenets of Black Feminist theory is the idea that by sharing knowledge of their experiences, women become collectively more conscious of their situation

Occurring around the same time that Robert Johnson was alive, the Harlem Renaissance was a geographical phenomenon where stable family relationships as well as creative artistic expression were able to coexist. It was the black culture's artistic explosion in the Harlem district of

New York City. This element of having a stable location allowed artists who were involved in the Harlem Renaissance to live more traditional lifestyles than the artists who participated in the blues culture of the South. As shown in The Search for Robert Johnson, blues artists depended on their ability to travel from city to city to support their occupations. This mobility factor caused them to be subject to a private lifestyle that was single and unattached. The majority of the artists in the Harlem Renaissance were New York transplants, meaning they moved to the city from the South. Before living in the city, many of them were migrant farmers and field hands and had a history of practicing a more traditional married lifestyle. They brought their family values with them when they moved to Harlem, and for the first time the community at large found it acceptable to choose an artistic profession, as they married and established stable private lives.

The majority of the artists in the Harlem Renaissance were New York transplants, meaning they moved to the city from the South.

Similarly, today's professional musicians and artists often marry and live traditional private lives. Jada Pinkett Smith and Will Smith are prime examples of two well-known entertainment professionals who have been able to establish a working relationship while pursuing their individual careers. During the blues and jazz era the entertainment workforce majority consisted of African American men. There were few women—such as Billy

Holiday—who participated in this cultural benchmark. The magnitude of women's involvement is maximized in modern times. The increase of women allowed for an increase in marriage and inter-relationships in that field. These women were familiar with the unusual circumstances and elements that accompany the lifestyle of an entertainer.

The hierarchy of the modern day sports profession requires most athletes to play college-level prior to advancing to a professional league. While in college, young athletes are able to meet with other members of their socio-economic class,

The formal introduction of the higher education system as a prerequisite to a sports profession particularly benefits the African American community.

and often establish relationships and eventually marry. The formal introduction of the higher education system as a prerequisite to a sports profession particularly benefits the African American community. Scholarships are provided to lower class African Americans who otherwise would not have the opportunity to attend college. Eventually they earn their degree and enter the professional work force. Thus, their social status improves regardless of whether they turn professional or not.

Indeed, African American professional artists and athletes have come a long way since the blues era. Today the fields of entertainment and sports are some of the most sought after professions. The individuals in these professions more than match the definition of the "Talented Tenth" as put forth by W.E.B. DuBois.

The next step for the African American community is to establish avenues for entertainers and sports professionals to invest their wealth into developing businesses in predominately black neighborhoods, thus bringing prosperity back to the community and ultimately building a base for successful black-owned businesses in fields other than entertainment and sports. Hank Aaron's successful ventures with Church's Chicken franchises are a prime example of this theory. Magic Johnson, formally of the Los Angeles Lakers, has recently launched a number of business ventures, including a chain of Starbucks, which are targeted towards black communities across the country.

> By setting up a system for successful entertainers and athletes to reinvest in the African American community, these firms could help to bridge the gap between the upper class and the middle class.

It is time that we move forward with unified efforts to allow more entertainers and sports professionals to follow in the footsteps of Hank and Magic. We should establish investment firms that target African Americans, to help facilitate investments between wealthy African Americans and educated businessmen. By setting up a system for successful entertainers and athletes to reinvest in the African American community, these firms could help to bridge the gap between the upper class and the middle class. Jobs would be created that benefit the lower class workforce. It's a win/win situation for all parties involved, supporting upward mobility while allowing work for the lower status labor force; truly, this theory can be considered a combination of the thoughts documented by both Booker T. Washington and W.E.B. DuBois.

Essay 2

The Harlem Renaissance

Fire:
> 1. A chemical reaction, especially the burning of a combustible substance with oxygen that releases heat and light;
> 2. To cause to ignite or become ignited;
> 3. To arouse the emotions of.

Fire can melt down the strongest of substances, like the melting of racist attitudes into respect. Fire burns and blazes, leaving undeniable effects, like the impact that the Harlem Renaissance had on American history. Fire gives light, like the inspiration that shines in the mind of people who read the collective works published by the Niggerati. In November of 1926, Langston Hughes, Zora Neale Hurston, John Preston Davis, Gwendolyn Bennett, Wallace Thurman, Aaron Douglas, and Bruce Nugent, as members of the black intelligentsia group Niggerati, published the one and only issue of *Fire!!* Education was the element that made the Niggerati truly unique. All of the authors of *Fire!!* had some form of higher education, and it is this meld of higher education and economical empowerment that helped the Harlem Renaissance bloom.

Education was the element that made the Niggerati truly unique.

The Niggerati existed during the Reconstruction era, the time in American history immediately following the abolishment of slavery. For the first time African Americans were allowed to earn their own wages, establish businesses, and begin to build a solid financial foundation for their community. However, the African American community was a new development, and the financial structure was just beginning to form. Excess cash to invest in cultural endeavors and leisure activities like the arts was not available. Young African American artists of the time looked to major organizations, like the NAACP, or the more endowed white community, to fund their works. The white investors and the NAACP often censored the work that they financed. By independently funding *Fire!!* the Niggerati empowered themselves and created a vehicle where they could maintain artistic control. Unfortunately, self-financing would turn out to be a double-edged sword, as the collaborative efforts of the group quickly ran out of funds and the paper folded after the first issue. What a shame that such a paper does not still exist as an uninhibited and uncensored platform to express the thoughts of the African American intelligentsia.

> The white investors and the NAACP often censored the work that they financed.

* * *

The Harlem Renaissance was an artistic and cultural explosion theoretically contained in Harlem, New York City, but having national repercussions and effects.

The fact that the artists in the Harlem Renaissance had such long careers is a direct result of the family values that existed in this era. Because the community respected an artist's lifestyle choices, they were more capable of focusing solely on their work. The Harlem community itself became the supporters of artists, creating a market for African American artwork and contributing to the longevity and stability of an artist's career. All the members of the Niggerati who worked on Fire!! established productive and successful careers for themselves; Langston Hughes and Zora Neale Hurston went on to become world-renowned and highly acclaimed writers, and Gwendolyn Bennett became a professor of the arts. The prosperity of these young artists lives can largely be contributed to the respect and support that they received from the common African American community.

PART 3:

Philosophy and Linguistics

Essay 1

Ethics, Morals, and a "Just Life"

The dialogues of Plato form the foundation for much of modern philosophy, expounding on a range of topics from reality and morality to justice and theories of governance. These essays are written in a dialogue form now known as "the Socratic method," as it was generally Plato's mentor Socrates who served as the mouthpiece of the central philosophy for each essay.

The Republic is considered Plato's best, wherein he poses the idea of Philosopher Kings to rule justly and without tyranny; it also contains the famous "Allegory of the Cave." Plato's ideas of how to frame a just government also reflect how an individual may live their life justly. He postulates that a just life must contain four main virtues: wisdom, courage, moderation/temperance, and justice. While the element of intellect is governed by wisdom, the spirit harbors one's courage. And while moderation maintains balance, it is justice which combines and strengthens the three other virtues and dictates a truly just life. Plato outlines the types of governments in Book VIII of *The Republic*, paralleling a city-state government with an individual's personality. The types of government are that of a philosopher king, a timocracy (where rank is based on honor), an oligarchy (where power is limited to an elite group), a democracy (where government is of the people, by the people), and a tyranny. A philosopher uses wisdom and his understanding

> While the element of intellect is governed by wisdom, the spirit harbors one's courage.

of justice—a concept which only a philosopher can truly understand—to guide his rule. Courage governs a timocracy, whereas desire for wealth and power dominates the rule of an oligarchy. A democracy, Plato postulates, is a government with the solitary goal of freedom, at the expense of all else. A tyranny is a government devoid of law or justice. In Plato's view, once an individual reaches the level of tyranny they have become a beast and are totally at the whim of spontaneous desires. This is an individual and a government that is a prisoner to unlawful and lustful yearnings.

> ... Plato makes the statement that an unjust life can be mathematically quantified ...

In Book IX of *The Republic*, Plato presents a number of reasons as to why a just life is a happier state than an unjust life. One of these reasons is the tyrant's very lifestyle lacking all reason, which leads him to seek only instant gratification, plunging him into debt, thievery, and ultimately despair. Having proven that, Plato makes the statement that an unjust life can be mathematically quantified, based on the gradation between the five types of government and the intervals between happiness and the tyrant. Plato explains that a just soul is 729 times happier than an unjust soul, and vice versa, because of the differences of the successive "governments" that stand between them.

Images are the elements in life that can be used to most influence the soul. Images can diminish or enhance the harmony of one's life. In Book VII of *The Republic*, Plato describes his theory of 'the divided line.' He discusses the objects of perception as shadows, physical objects, mathematical objects, and ideas. Conjecture leads from shadows to physical. Conviction proceeds to mathematical understanding and ultimately leads us to thoughts and ideas. Dialect is essential to an individual reaching the section of the line that involves ideas and forms. The perception of ideas and images are called forms, and are central to Plato's philosophy attempting to explain reality. Fully understanding the Form of the Good—and thus leading a just life—would place one on the highest point of the line.

In the famous "Allegory of the Cave," Plato sets up a hypothetical situation wherein a group of people has been raised in a cave without ever having seen daylight; in fact, they are all chained and bound in such a way that they can only stare directly ahead at the cave wall before them. Behind them is a fire, and in between the prisoners and the fire is a walkway. The fire casts shadows on the wall of the cave as various statues and objects are carried across the walkway, and the prisoners then name and guess what the objects are and mean. This becomes a game to them, and the ability to recognize and decode the shadows with speed and accuracy becomes the basis of the only hierarchy they have, and the foundation of their society. The situation then changes, and a prisoner is released from bounds and freed from the cave. After his eyes get used to the bright light of the sun, the prisoner realizes that the shadows were merely representations of other objects, and not actually objects themselves. The prisoner then would return to the cave to free the others. However, when he did return to the dark of the cave, he would not be able to see as well or play the game of shadows, which is all his fellow prisoners know. The fellow prisoners would believe that his eyesight had been ruined by being outside, and they could lose the only station they have in life should they too be freed. Plato contends that the prisoners would refuse freedom, resisting even possible murder. Thus, Plato is presenting the problem that keeps so many from seeing the truth, resisting seeing even when the truth is right in front of them.

> Plato is presenting the problem that keeps so many from seeing the truth, resisting seeing even when the truth is right in front of them.

In Book II of *The Republic*, Glaucon, in an attempt to get Socrates to explain what makes justice desirable in and of itself over injustice, relates the "Ring of Gyges" myth. He begins by saying, "The test I propose makes the assumption that both the just and the unjust enjoy the peculiar liberty said to have been granted to Gyges" (Rep. 359d). Glaucon then goes on to explain the myth: Gyges was a shepherd who served the King of Lydia. One day while he was feeding his sheep, a storm came and a huge cavern opened in the ground. Upon descending into the cavern, Gyges found a hollow bronze horse. Inside the horse was a naked dead man who wore a gold ring. Gyges took the ring and exited the cavern. He later found out the ring had the power to make him invisible when he turned the stone inward. In light of the new power that he possessed with the ring, Gyges managed to have himself appointed to the King's court, seduced the queen, killed the existing King, and became the King of Lydia. Glaucon's opinion is that the story of the Ring of Gyges is an example of justice being the third type of good, but only good for its effects. He says, "No man is so unyielding that he would remain obedient to justice and keep his hands off what does not belong to him if he could steal with impunity in the very midst of the public market itself" (Rep. 260b). By this he means that people only act just out of fear of the repercussions if they were to be caught acting otherwise. If we all had an opportunity like Gyges, we would employ unjust tactics to fulfill our selfish interests.

> *Glaucon's opinion is that the story of the Ring of Gyges is an example of justice being the third type of good, but only good for its effects.*

The Egoist school of thought has elements that support Glaucon's point of view. In an article titled "Egoism and Moral Skepticism", James Rachels speaks of human nature, saying, "If we want to persuade him to act decently toward his fellow humans, we will have to make our appeal to such other attitudes as he does possess, by threats, bribes, or other cajolery" (*Right & Wrong*, p.190). Rachels agrees with Plato, and believes that the fear of punishment is the only thing that influences humans to act justly and maintain order in society.

A fundamental component of Egoist theory is the act of promoting others to behave as altruists, while personally advocating self-interest. This particular method of action parallels the ring in the myth of Gyges. The ability to publicly appear one way while personally supporting other interests allows the Egoist's selfish intentions to go undetected by society. Like the ring, it enables them to be invisible. Based on the above ideology, Glaucon's hypothesis of what would happen if there were two rings is wrong. He says, "The just man would act no differently from the unjust" (Rep. 360c). From the Egoist perspective, the unjust individual with a ring would promote all others to be altruists, thus persuading the just individual who has a ring to behave in a manner that perpetuates common interest. This would then only allow opportunity for the unjust man to act on self-interests as Gyges did.

> *A fundamental component of Egoist theory is the act of promoting others to behave as altruists, while personally advocating self-interest.*

The teachings of Kant involve theories that undermine Glaucon's interpretation of the "Ring of Gyges" myth. Kantianism looks at the morals and good-natured behavior that determine an individual's action. It is a science that identifies laws and formulas for making moral decisions, and centers on the belief that humans are ends that should be exempt from being considered means for others' intentions. This supports the idea of justice as being the first type of good, in that it is only good in and of itself. Based on Kantianism, even though Gyges had the ability to be invisible, he should have conducted himself in accordance with ethical laws and refrained from conspiring to kill the king. In theory, Kantianism seems like a more ethical school of thought but in practice it proves to be flawed. The ring represents an opportunity for Gyges to change his current circumstances. What if, as a shepherd, he dreamed of being able to improve his social and economic status? When in possession of the ring, is he expected to abandon his hopes and dreams for the sake of upholding the ideals of moral laws? In an article titled "A Critique of Kantianism", Richard Taylor comments, "Ends in Themselves are, thus, not to be thought of as those men that live and toil on earth"(*Right & Wrong* p.67). Kantianism leaves no room for consideration of human emotions in determining one's actions. It implies that in order for someone to be just they must sacrifice their individual aspirations, even if it means suffering.

In theory, Kantianism seems like a more ethical school of thought but in practice it proves to be flawed.

W.T. Stace says, "The ethical relativist claims that there are no objective moral standards: right and wrong vary from culture to culture"(*Right & Wrong* p.142). In short, this means that ethical relativists are people who have the fundamental belief that individuals of various collective groups should determine what is moral and immoral for themselves. In 1934, at the age of 47, Ruth Benedict wrote *A Defense of Ethical Relativism*; in it, she shares her opinion that normality is culturally defined. She explains that "No one civilization can possibly utilize in its mores the whole potential range of human behavior" (*Right & Wrong*, p.139). Ethical relativists do not contend that there is one universal force that governs the lives of the masses. They prefer to believe that it is the actual "right" of the individual groups to determine what is good for their own society. The extreme degree of the ethical relativist perspective holds that to interfere with one's behavior is an actual violation of one's human rights. It seems that the basis for this theory can be traced back to the first Greek, a Western historian named Herodotus. Herodotus lived before Plato, from 484 B.C.– 425 B.C. He believed that everyone, without exception, thinks that their own native customs are better than all others.

> *Ethical relativists do not contend that there is one universal force that governs the lives of the masses.*

Essay 2

The Evolution of Swahili

The Swahili language is the most popular language of sub-Saharan Africa. It is a bold language spoken primarily along the northeastern coast of Africa, and the three countries that use Swahili as their official language form the eastern coast. Swahili has a strong connection to the Arabic culture and people because of Arab trade routes.

Swahili in its basic structure and development represents the African version of the English language. Swahili is comprised primarily of a large number of borrowed words from Arabic, Asian and European languages, built on the native Bantu tongue. Some who would contend that Swahili is primarily from the Arabic root, especially since the specific root of the actual word swahili comes from the Arabic for "coast." Linguists, however, have determined that the basic language structure and vocabulary of Swahili is most certainly Bantu in origin, and shares little with Arabic beyond a large number of borrowed words. After all, the amount of loaner words in Swahili from Arabic language is similar to the amount of French, Latin, and Greek in English. And just as in the English culture when one uses French words, the more Arabic words in Swahili that one uses is considered a mark of a higher level of language. This is not a measure of culture to say that one culture is better than the other; rather this argument is made to illustrate the dynamics of language. Swahili is the official language

> *Linguists, however, have determined that the basic language structure and vocabulary of Swahili is most certainly Bantu in origin.*

spoken in Tanzania, Kenya, and Uganda. As such, it is the first language for some five million Africans, and the second language spoken by almost thirty to fifty million people in Mozambique, Rwanda, Somalia, and South Africa. Swahili is spoken the world over, including in the United States. The influence that the Arab traders had on Swahili, while not as extensive as once thought, can still be seen. In 1728, a Swahili manuscript was discovered, an epic poem written in the Arabic script. The writing system has since become the Latin alphabet because of influence from European colonization, where administrative tasks—which during the era of colonialism were positions of power in Africa—were written in one of the Romance languages.

Although the language of Swahili is heavily influenced by the trade with Arabian nations, the culture is purely African. One would think that with the large amount of trading that went on between the two cultures (and which still goes on today) some of their artifacts would be exchanged, though this does hold true in the case of religion, since so many of the Africans that speak Swahili are Muslim. Take for example, the superstitious belief of some Swahili-speaking African Muslims who bathe in Koran-soaked water to cure ailments. The Swahili are a superstitious culture, as evidenced by this quote from Africa Online: "Swahili believe in spirits (djinns). Most men wear protective amulets around their necks, which contain verses from the Koran." (*Art*, 2)

What else is different about the countries that call Swahili their native language? A sign of wealth is an old carved door made out of wood. Such things as these are evidence that their original culture is still valued in today's times. Speaking of time, the time system is different in Swahili countries. It runs from dawn to dusk, rather than from midnight to midday, and 7 in the morning and 7 in the evening are considered their one o'clock. At 7 AM one would say saa moja asubuni, which translates into "hour one morning."

The time system is different in Swahili countries. It runs from dawn to dusk, rather than from midnight to midday.

The thing that is difficult about Swahili is the class system that lies in the basic grammatical and syntactical structure of the Bantu language. Historically, the Bantu language had 22 noun classes, but today there are fourteen. An example of this class system, just one of many, is the pairing of a prefix with a nominal stem, a noun form that requires a suffix or prefix to form a true noun. Unlike English, where a suffix alone denotes a plural, Swahili has two different prefixes for each case. There are twenty-nine consonants and five vowels are Swahili. The consonants are: a e I o o b c d dh f g gh h j k l m n ng ng' p r s sh t th w y z. The language also has dialects spoken in the different regions and nations that it calls home. For example, Kiunguja is the dialect spoken in Zanzibar, and was chosen by colonial administrators to be the "base" for standard Swahili.

The numeric counting system in Swahili reflects the Arabic influence. "Sita" is six, "saba" is seven, and "tisa" is nine, all of which were words borrowed from the Arabic language. However the rest of the numbers are based on Bantu words, such as "moja" for one, "tatu" for three, "nne" for four, "tano" for five, "nane" for eight, and "kumi" for ten. Thus can be seen the natural assimilation between the different languages of Asia and Africa.

The two cultures are so interrelated that Africans in other countries on the continent often debate or question whether the language and culture of Swahili can be truly considered African. Some purists still contend that the language is more Arabic than African and that it should not be used or accepted as readily as it is. In this modern age there is a movement going on across the African continent pushing Africans to return to their original tribal languages. These people would like to see colonial languages such as French, German, and English phased out in favor of the traditional tribal languages. While it is relatively simple to make the distinction between the original African cultures and their colonial invaders, the line becomes blurry in the case of Swahili. There is less of a stigma involved with the Arabic trade routes that spread Islam and Persian influence, and it occurred over a much longer period of time.

Indeed, Swahili is a prolific language and is certainly not limited to the East African countries where it is primarily

> Some purists still contend that the language is more Arabic than African and that it should not be used or accepted as readily as it is.

spoken. International radio stations BBC and Voice of America broadcast programs in Swahili; Swahili is also the basis for the increasingly popular but relatively young holiday, Kwanzaa. Kwanzaa comes from the Swahili word for "first harvest," and was founded by the African American nationalist Ron Karenga, and first celebrated from December 26, 1966, to January 1, 1967. The holiday starts the day after Christmas and lasts for seven days, with each day representing a different principle, or Nguzo Saba. The seven principles of Kwanzaa are umoja (unity), kujichagulia (self-determination), ujima (collective work and responsibility), ujamaa (cooperative economics), nia (purpose), kuumba (creativity), and imani (faith). Kwanzaa is practiced as a secular holiday by thousands in this country. The ceremony for this non-religious holiday includes pouring libations and the lighting of the seven candles (one for each of the seven principles).

Swahili is the basis for the increasingly popular but relatively young holiday, Kwanzaa.

Swahili went mainstream, and Hollywood, in the 1994 Disney film *The Lion King*. In the movie, the phrase "hakuna matata" is used, which in Swahili literally means "no problems." Also, the characters Simba and Rafiki owe their names to Swahili, meaning "lion" and "friend", respectively. Likewise, to represent the globalization of Swahili, safari is the word for "journey."

As can be seen, the African language of Swahili is a mature and fully evolved language, thriving in today's globalized world. Despite the questions of Swahili's authenticity as a traditional African language, it is nevertheless in widespread use and shows no signs of slowing. Its syntactical structure is uniquely African, and the Arabic influence is a product of the beginnings of globalization, where trade and communication between cultures and countries increase. In the coming years, Swahili will no doubt be the language of the African nations, as countries organize politically and economy, addressing their shortfalls and realizing they have the resources to evolve into major players on the global stage.

PART 4:

Anthropology

Essay 1

A Brief History of Homo sapiens

The development of adaptive strategies for humans evolved throughout time. It has taken millions of years of development for us to form into the people that we are today. Let's take time to discuss the stages through which humans have developed and explore the impact that various discoveries have had on mankind.

About five million years ago the hominid Ardipithecus ramidus emerged.

The earliest stage of human-like animals, referred to as hominids, walked the earth about six million years ago. This creature was ape-like and called *Orrorin tugenensis*, and links the human species to the oldest ancestor common between humans and apes, where the two species separated genetically. About five million years ago the hominid *Ardipithecus ramidus* emerged. This animal stood approximately four feet tall and also may have walked upright on two feet. Walking primarily on two feet is one of the main characteristics in classifying hominids. *Australopithecus anamensis* is the name of the hominid that walked the earth a mere four million years ago. The further bipedalism group that walked the earth were *A. Afarensis*, *A. Africanus*, and the *A. Bosei*, inhabiting the earth approximately three million years ago.

About two million years ago the fossil record indicates an advanced species *Homo habilis*. Many of these fossils were found with or near primitive tools, and thus are considered the earliest example of the hunter and gatherer society. Women were the gatherers and farmers, while the men were hunters. The discovery and creation of tools had a huge impact on the lives of the *Homo habilis,* allowing them to better tear and eat meat. Contemporary scientists theorize that the mating practices of these animals were most likely an alpha male system.

> The discovery and creation of tools had a huge impact on the lives of the **Homo habilis.**

Homo erectus was the hominids that walked the earth one million years ago, and structurally represents the shift toward the larger braincase and receding brow ridge characteristic of modern humans. H. erectus lived to be about thirty years old. During this time, the orientation of tools advanced to be Acheulean, or carved stone tools. It is theorized that H. erectus was the first hominid to use fire, although the truth to this theory has been extremely hard to prove. Fire purified the meats so that people lived longer and died less of disease. At night, other animals were chased away with fire and thus the dark of night was conquered. Another major development that strengthened in this age was sexual fidelity and pair bonding.

The *Homo neanderthalensis,* better known as Neanderthal, developed about three hundred thousand years ago. This species developed larger brains than its predecessors, and co-existed with our species, the Homo sapiens.

* * *

There is a reason why for thousands of years men have been the dominant sex, just as there are reasons why for millions of years humans have been the dominant species on this planet. Here we will explore the many significant differences between males and females as well as examine what makes humans the primary species on the earth.

By nature women are talkers, and contemporary anthorologists theorize that this developed out a women's need to educate her children. Women generally stand in circles to talk, while men scatter to farm and hunt. Men are quieter because they were historically the hunters or farmers, and thus, they were more prone to use the spatial reasoning portions of their brain. Another difference, obviously, is that women give birth, and during their nine months of pregnancy, with a limited range of movement, become dependent on their mate for support.

> *Women give birth, and during their nine months of pregnancy, with a limited range of movement, become dependent on their mate for support.*

Besides the invention of tools and the use of fire, it is the intellect of *H. sapiens* that has made human beings the ultimate primate on this planet. The capacity to solve problems and adapt quickly and efficiently to new environments is what sets humans apart from other animals. Humans have spread across the face of this planet from the frozen plains of Antarctica, the blistering heat of the Sahara Desert, the stretch of the oceans, and, even further than the confines of our planet, in our continuing exploration of space.

Essay 2

Culture Clashes in Globalization

There are many immigrant families living in Europe who have had to adjust to living among a different culture, and have had experiences where their culture clashes with European culture. One of the most prevalent cultural clashes is in the area of child rearing. For example, in Romania, where the Gypsy population has existed for a thousand years after emigrating from India, it is a Gypsy tradition to have arranged marriages. Between the ages of 14 and 16 girls are usually forced to marry a young man, usually as part of a monetary transaction. The parents choose who the man will be. However, much of Europe does not practice arranged marriages, and find this practice outdated and offensive. The Gypsy people look at arranged marriages as a healthy and reasonable way of life because they put so much money and care into raising their daughters, who will not otherwise be able to work and support the family. Thus, as they see it, without arranged marriage the family would not see a return on the time and money that they invested. Boys are viewed as different, as they are able to earn a living and bring income to the household.

> Much of Europe does not practice arranged marriages, and find this practice outdated and offensive.

* * *

Child rearing in America has become a billion dollar industry. By the time a baby is one year old, the child's parents will have had to buy a car seat, a crib, a changing table, a playpen, a stroller, piles of clothing, 2,000-plus diapers, toys, hundreds of cans of formula and jars of strained foods, as well as wipes, swabs, shampoos, ointments, and the like. By the time a baby who was born in the year 2000 is six, his or her family will have spent a daunting $97,762 on the child's upbringing. Parents earning $64,000 or more will have spent $300,000 by the child's eighteenth birthday. As a result of the financial burden of child rearing in America, many parents are forced to budget even more dollars for child care services.

* * *

Different cultures have different marital beliefs and practices. Some cultures practice polygyny (practice of having more than one wife or female mate at a time) while others practice polyandry (practice of having more than one husband or male mate at a time). Only about 16 percent of 185 worldwide cultures restrict marriage to monogamy, as ours does. This reading examines various types of marriage and delves into why one form would work in a given culture yet not work at all in another.

> Only about 16 percent of 185 worldwide cultures restrict marriage to monogamy, as ours does.

A symbolic marriage is the type of marriage a nun would have with Christ. The nun is not allowed to have relations with other men, nor is she allowed to marry anyone else. And although the nun does not have sex, this is not considered a non-sexual marriage. Non-sexual marriages are usually marriages that take place for money. Love is a cultural choice and sometimes does not come into consideration in non-sexual marriages.

Other types of marriages are fixed-term marriages that are under contract and last for a certain period of time. There are also group marriages that are a communal gathering; homosexual marriages between members of the same gender; and mentor marriages where an older person marries a younger to help with financial resources.

> *Oftentimes I talk about wanting to have children and forget to mention the aspect of getting married first...*

In my own family, marriage was not a primary focus. My mother had two children and never married, instead deciding to focus on law school. She made a very good lawyer, but was never married. She says now that she is retired she would like to get married. My mother's decision not to marry had a big impact on me. Oftentimes I talk about wanting to have children and forget to mention the aspect of getting married first; perhaps it's because I have experienced a comfortable middle class lifestyle without the income of two parents.

* * *

Religion is one of the most important areas of life. It deals with ones' belief in the supernatural, metaphysics, death, health, and money. Almost all aspects of life are touched by religion. In this reading, we will examine religion in Ecuador, in Gabon in western Africa, as well as that of the

Toraja people. After outlining each group's religious practices, we can determine how their religion affects what they do and how they live their lives.

The people of Ecuador were colonized under the Catholic banner, meaning they were forced to attend Mass and to adopt Catholic practices. Although the people of Ecuador were forced to make a transition to Catholicism, they still maintain some traditional religious ways. Their traditional religious practices were animism, or the belief that nature is made up of spirits. They would pray to the forces of the mountain and the sun. They also believed that nature held healing powers. As a result they often used Shamans, spiritual herbs, and medicine people to heal the sick. Their Shamans were said to walk between two worlds—that of the living and that of the dead. The way in which the Ecuadorian people mixed their old religious values with their new Roman Catholic beliefs demonstrates their ability to be creative when faced with adversity. Their mixed religion sets a base for other actions; there are other examples that they do that are a mixture of old and new. For example, they create their traditional old crafts and sell them on the new European market.

> *Although the people of Ecuador were forced to make a transition to Catholicism, they still maintain some traditional religious ways.*

The Toraja people are indigenous to the mountainous regions of South Sulawesi, Indonesia. In their culture, family ties are considered paramount, lasting even after death. In the eyes of a Torajan, the only division between life and death is marked by the funeral ceremony; indeed, the funeral is considered the most important ceremony of one's life, and as such, an extremely highly-valued—and expensive—event. When someone dies they are considered to be sick or sleeping until the funeral can take place. This could be years, for the funeral ceremony is not held until all family members can come together and save enough to make it a proper funeral, so as not to disrespect the spirit of their relative. After the funeral ceremony the men of the village carry the dead body out into the mountains where the body will reside in cliff-side vaults. The Toraja people's religious practices call for patience and strength, and places heavy importance on family and community. Though the population now largely identifies as Protestant, they have still maintained most aspects of their beliefs despite the synthesis that has occurred between the two belief structures.

The Gabon people of West Africa also practice a Catholic religion that is mixed with their traditional culture. This is different from the people of Ecuador because it is not mixed with their traditional religion, just their culture, being seen in aspects of their language, songs, costumes, and instruments. In the Catholic ceremonies of the Gabon people, all of these West African cultural aspects are present, rather than the traditional Catholic ones seen in most Catholic ceremonies. For the Gabon people their religion

The Toraja people's religious practices call for patience and strength, and places heavy importance on family and community.

affects everything that they do, and like their religion, their modern practices are very westernized.

Bibliography

Ali, Hassan O. "Swahili Language & Culture." 5 February 2006.
http://www.glcom.com/hassan/swahili_history.html

Annenberg Media. Briding World History: Early Economies, Unit 8. Accessed October 26, 2006.
http://www.learner.org/channel/courses/worldhistory/unit_video_8-1.html

Art & Life in Africa Online. "Swahili Information."
5 February 2006.
http://www.uiowa.edu/africart/toc/people/Swahili.htm

Blackmaon, Robert. *Medieval Sourcebook: The Golden Legend.* 29 September 2001.
http://www.fordham.edu/halsall/basis/goldenlegend/GL-voll-golgenlegend.html

Cunningham, Lawrence S. "Legends For Their Times."
Commonwealth. Vol 121, Issue 10. 20 May 1994. 40–43.

Derbes, Anne and Mark Sandona. "Barren metal and the Fruitful Womb: The Program of Giotto's Arena Chapel in Padua." Art Bulletin. Vol. 80 Issue 2. June 1998. 274–292.

Jacobus, Laura. "Giotto's Annunciation in the Arena Chapel, Padua." Art Bulletin. Vol. 81, Issue 1. March 1999. 93108.

Kosanji Temple Museum. Accessed October 27, 2006.
http://www.kousanji.or.jp/etop.htm

Kren, Emil and Marx, Daniel. "Biography: Giotto di Bondone."
Web Gallery of Art. 29 September 2001.
http://gallery.euroweb.hu/bio/g/giotto/biograph.html

Maldari, Donald C. "Book Reviews." *America: The Catholic Weekly Magazine*. Vol. 171, Issue 11. 15 October 1994. 26–28.

McClester, Cedric. *Kwanzaa: Everything You Always Wanted To Know But Didn't Know Where To Ask*. Gumbs & Thomas Publishing: New York. 1990.

Microsoft Encarta Online Encyclopedia 2001. "Giotto." 29 September 2001.
http://encarta.msn.com/find/Concise.asp?ti=05652000

Murphy, Declan. "Byoudoin, The Phoenix Pavilian." The Yamasa Institute. 1 July 2002.
http://www.yamasa.org/japan/english/destination/kyoto/byoudoin.html

NNDB.com. "Giotto di Bondone." Accessed November 3, 2006.
http://www.nndb.com/people/703/000084451/

Omniglot. "A Guide to Written Language." 5 February 2006.
http://www.omniglot.com/writing/swahili.htm

PBS. "The Evolution Project: Human Evolution." Accessed November 3, 2006.
http://www.pbs.org/wgbh/evolution/humans/humankind/c.html

Plato. "The Republic." Translated by G.M.A. Grube, with revisions by C.D.C. Reeve. Indianapolis: Hackett Publishing, 1992.

Reames, Sherry L. Book Reviews. *Church History*. Vol. 64, Issue 1. March 1995. 98–101.

Reese, Lyn. "Female Heroes of the Regions of the World: Murasaki Shikibu." *Women in World History Curriculum*. 1 July 2002.
http://www.womeninworldhistory.com/heroine9.html

Sacred Destinations Travel Guide. Accessed October 26, 2006.
http://www.sacred-destinations.com/japan/kyoto-byodoin.htm

Satoshi, Yabuuchi. "The Great Buddhist Sculptor, Jocho."
1 July 2002.
http://wwww3.big.or.jp/~yabus/museE.html.data/Essay%20Corner/Jocho.html

Wikipedia. "Cappella degli Scrovegni." Accessed November 3, 2006.
http://en.wikipedia.org/wiki/Arena_Chapel

—. "Swahili Language." 5 February 2006.
http://en.wikipedia.org/wiki/Swahili

—. "Fujiwara Clan." Accessed October 25, 2006.
http://en.wikipedia.org/wiki/Fujiwara_clan

—. "Murasaki Shikibu." Accessed October 25, 2006.
http://en.wikipedia.org/wiki/Murasaki_Shikibu

—. "Robert Johnson." Accessed November 2, 2006.
http://en.wikipedia.org/wiki/Robert_Johnson

www.ingramcontent.com/pod-product-compliance
Lightning Source LLC
Chambersburg PA
CBHW031643170426
43195CB00035B/563